Lydia Michael was born and raised in a small town in Nicosia, Cyprus. From a young age, she was fascinated by her parents' stories of the countryside lifestyle, working abroad, meeting people from around the world, and even fighting in a war. As she grew older, she decided to explore the world and see different perspectives on life. So, at 18, her life story of traveling and living abroad started. Nowadays, she works as a freelance travel writer and shares poetry to help others creatively visualize life.

Lydia Michael

# LADY MOON

AUSTIN MACAULEY PUBLISHERS™
LONDON · CAMBRIDGE · NEW YORK · SHARJAH

Copyright © Lydia Michael 2023

The right of Lydia Michael to be identified as author of this work has been asserted by the author in accordance with sections 77 and 78 of the Copyright, Designs and Patents Act 1988.

All rights reserved. No part of this publication may be reproduced, stored in a retrieval system, or transmitted in any form or by any means, electronic, mechanical, photocopying, recording, or otherwise, without the prior permission of the publishers.

Any person who commits any unauthorised act in relation to this publication may be liable to criminal prosecution and civil claims for damages.

A CIP catalogue record for this title is available from the British Library.

ISBN 9781035804771 (Paperback)
ISBN 9781035804788 (ePub e-book)

www.austinmacauley.com

First Published 2023
Austin Macauley Publishers Ltd®
1 Canada Square
Canary Wharf
London
E14 5AA

# Free

A small countryside town
A house of olive trees and vines
A family of love and happiness

Golden wheat fields spread out
Colourful wildflowers paint the streets
Yellow daisies sing happily in the sun

Recklessly I run in the fields
My shepherd dog, my only companion
I feel free and wild

It's a blissful ambience
A carefree life
I feel free and wild

I am a free spirit
Looking for freedom.

# Freedom

Freedom,
A favourite blessing
The biggest desire

I was never locked up in any kind of way
I never had to run away
I never had to fight for my freedom

Raised in a lovely home
Doting parents,
Protective siblings,
Lovable friends.

Still, I wanted to be free.

A young child,
An idealistic world
I never had to overthink
I never had to over analyse my actions

As I grew,
I realised some freedoms,
Were not understood
Neither seen by kids

Or so I thought

As a child, I always adored tigers
But I never expressed the desire to be a tiger,
I always wanted to be a bird.

A tiger is strong and independent
And that's what I've always wanted to be
That's what my parents taught me to be

But a bird can fly freely in the sky
It can go wherever it wants
And escape from undesired situations

Kids do not realise the weight the word freedom holds

The simple wish to be yourself without any reservations

The desire to do, whatever you wish to do, without being judged
These seem normal to a kid
But so complicated to an adult

Society creates expectations
A destined path
A specific road

However, sometimes that path is just not the one we want.
Now I know, I always wanted to be a bird so I could fly away

So, I dreamed of having wings
And flying away to any place I wanted.

# Different Path

A small island
In between three continents
Diverse culture
But not a diverse country

Tiny country but rich in history
A history of war and grief
A history of sadness
But also a history of brave fighters

Fighting for love
Fighting for justice
Fighting for freedom

But, while looking for freedom,
People lost their humanity

Living on an island
Surrounded by water
Enslaved by land

People forgot what is beyond
They became one clan, one family, one story
There was only one perspective

But I wanted to have my story

I chose to follow my story
To see other perspectives

I want to become part of different worlds
Different movements
Different dimensions

I want to go on a different path.

# Flying Away

Cotton-shaped clouds paint the sky
And the plane gets ready to fly high
I feel like a child excited by colourful candies
But I try hard to look fancy
I have my backpack, ripped jeans, and sunglasses on
And I am off to move on
The land is disappearing before my eyes
And my past life slowly dies

I don't know what to expect
Rainbows?
Clouds?
Rain?
Sunshine?

No matter what is coming towards me,
I feel ready to go into the unknown.

# Into the Unknown

Unexpected situations
Thrilling moments
Unknown lands

Even prepared,
you can't realise the massive differences the world has
Not until you see them

Today the world seems small
But it is in fact vast
So many countries, cultures, languages, and landscapes

Still, it is one thing to experience a different culture
And another to see a completely different earth
Our planet is truly beautiful

From endless golden wheat fields
To large oak trees, massive palm farms
To bottomless swamps and frozen lakes

Seeing the earth at its glory
Makes you feel insignificant
Makes you feel like the anonymous person you are.

# Anonymous

Walking alone on an unfamiliar lane
Sitting on a lonely bench on a crowded street
Having lunch at a small local café

Becoming a character of a street artist's painting
Blending in a colourful background
Being one with the crowd

As a traveller,
You get to blend in, to be like everyone else
To feel like a local in every place of the world

You gain miraculous superpowers
Like being able to just relax and enjoy
To absorb positiveness and feel free at anytime

As a solo traveller,
I got to seize the joy and beauty of anonymity
I can be anyone and follow the flow.

# The Flow

"When in Rome, do as the Romans do"

Travellers unconsciously follow the Romans
They become one with the locals
And they learn how to experience a different Rome

But life is like a never-ending roller coaster
Unexpected situations appear out of nowhere
Because that is the way of the flow

The journey for greater knowledge,
The desire to be part of a greater cause,
The trip for exploration and discovery can be scary

But I am a hopeless wanderer
Dreaming of moving with the flow
Following the tribe to a universal festival.

# Hopeless Wanderer

Wandering solo around the world,
living by myself abroad,
choosing to be single
A flaw in the matrix

Dreaming, exploring, discovering,
Learning and seizing life
Experiencing everything to the fullest
Too independent, too much of a dreamer

I am a hopeless wanderer
Wishing for the impossible
Doing the possible
Going beyond what I can see.

# Beyond

Ἄνθρωπος.
My favourite word in my language.

Ἄνθρωπος (Anthropos) means human.
But there is a deeper meaning behind it

Its true meaning is "seeing beyond".

Humans can see beyond what their eyes see.
Humans can think, analyse, research, conclude, and create.

From the beginning of time.
humans lived to explore

Journeying through life,
they go beyond their home, neighbourhood, city or country.
With every step, they achieve great milestones.

While travelling you see what incredible creatures humans can be
You see the amazing things they created and keep creating

With my first step as a traveller, I met inspiring people
Loving people
Carefree people
Ambitious people

And I chose to keep seeing beyond
To love, smile and dream
With the hope to create a life beyond my horizon.

# A Smile

A smile is a powerful tool
It's an asset for happiness, joy or contentment
It's an instigator for anger, jealousy or embarrassment

In a connected world
Friendships and relationships surpass borders
But misunderstandings will always be part of humanity

With a smile, I hope for understanding
I hope for forgiveness
I hope for acceptance

For a smile, I say thank you
For a smile, I keep giving
For a smile, I keep moving.

# Movement

As I move through life
I realise movement has many meanings
in any way you interpret it
it has a powerful impact.

When travelling
You are always on the move
And experience different movements

Some are simple
Like ordinary people going to work
Others create powerful 'movements'

A train takes you to any place you desire
It takes you away from your ordinary life, your dreadful environment or lethal routine,
Other times it takes you back home, to your family and friends.

A dancer's movements take you to different worlds,
they make you feel emotions you never experienced before,
and they give you powerful messages.

A person's movement gives away their lifestyle,
Or their personality and behaviour,
Or their hopes and dreams.

A social movement brings peace, understanding and hope,
It advocates for everyone's right to be able to move
And sometimes it forces you to stop and think

A person takes you to different dimensions
They move mountains or create storms
They move you with their love, their happiness or their rage and fear.

A movement is all about perspective
All you need is to choose your perspective.

# Perspective

I thought choosing a perspective would be easy
But travelling can also bring you a bitter taste

I thought everything would be rainbows and sunshine
But then I started seeing a cruel perspective

People couldn't see beyond
There was only anger, fear and hopelessness

It was an unwanted discovery
Realising the reality of the world, I felt hopeless

But I also felt guilty
Because I run away from it

I turned away from the grief
I kept moving, seeking life beyond the reality

Because I got scared by diversity
It felt loud and intense.

# Diversity

Love, kindness, understanding
Serenity, calmness. peace
So many virtues come with diversity

Hatred, cruelty, ignorance
Anxiety, violence, conflict
So many vices come with diversity

I'm trying so hard to see other perspectives
I'm fighting so hard other perspectives
And I wish I can see more perspectives

But instead, everyone is angry with me
Angry with my choices, my beliefs, my lifestyle
They only see what they want to see.

# A Sea

Like the waves, I dreamed of being free, wild and fierce
I wished to be unique
But they told me I was different because I was quiet and calm
I was just a sea

But I didn't get it
What was I lacking?
Why is my truth lesser than an ocean's when we are both bodies of water?

We may differ in some ways
Yet, we are still made by the same ingredients

I am so tired of being compared
All I ever wanted was to be me,
To be seen as who I am,
To be accepted

Whether I am a sea or an ocean,
I can have massive waves and sweep away anything that is in my way

Or, I can be calm, sweet and cheerful
It should be my choice and not the world's.

# Collapsing

The world was on the verge of collapsing
People lost their jobs, their homes, their hope

Living on the other side of the world
I was oblivious of the struggle

My family kept smiling
They wanted me to stay happy and confident

But I knew,
I knew things were going to be different

And I had no one else to blame but the world.

# The World

Couldn't the world be different?
Couldn't people be different?

I'm tired of living in this world

I want to have unforgettable moments
I want to see the real world
I want to see the world beyond the borders of my reality

I want to live extraordinary adventures,
Great emotional moments,
The satisfaction of doing what you desire, without any regrets

I want to live in a world where there are no unwritten rules
I want to create a world under my rules

Maybe, I'm the one who is different,
Everyone is happy with just what is around them
They feel fulfilment with only everything that is up to the horizon

Those around me are important to me
the horizon always greets me with a smile
But it's not enough
I want to see beyond the horizon.

# Human

Human, I'm scared of you
I'm scared to run, to play, to have fun
I'm scared
I don't know what to do
I don't know where to go
I see huge monsters
Nasty and horrific
I'm scared
I'm scared to talk, to dance, to dream
I'm scared to live, to laugh, to feel again
I'm scared
I'm trying to remember how it was before
When I used to feel joyous and carefree
When I was just a child.

# The People

A sacred place,
A place of philosophy, faith and resilience
Hundreds of people go there to marvel or pray
Monks pass in a slow, serene pace
In the corner, I see a group of young monks
They're holding a smartphone
They're watching a comedy show
They laugh loudly and cheerfully

A public space,
A space at a random corner shop on the street
Hundreds of people pass by it every day
A man lays in his sleeping bag trying to rest
He is alone and cold
Still, he's holding a smartphone
Watching a random video
He smiles tiredly

A busy place,
A place of travellers, thinkers and youth
Hundreds of people go there every day
A young girl sits comfortably at the couch

She is surrounded by strangers, but she feels safe
She is holding a smartphone
Watching a new Netflix series
She is happy and content

Three places, three people, three different experiences
I wonder whose smile is the real one.

# Every Day

Every day, people praise my beautiful smile
Every day, my friends complain about life's unfairness
I smile and comfort them saying how amazing life can be

But the truth is
I do not know how to deal with life
I'm miserable

Every day I put on a fake smile
I greet people with my most beautiful mask
and I try to deal with life in the best way I can

But it's not easy

I don't know why though
I have great friends for whom I would do anything
My family is loving and supportive

But deep down I'm lonely

I'm afraid to speak
I'm afraid to tell them about this feeling
I'm afraid of their reaction
I cry every night thinking I don't want to wake up

Every morning I'm forcing myself to continue with my day
I'm miserable

I think I lost myself
I don't know who I am anymore
I don't know what I'm fighting for
I lost all my ambitions and dreams

I need help,
I need someone to tell me, "It's okay if you are lost
You can still find your way
You are not alone, just grab my hand and I'll lead the way"

But that's only a dream.

# Dreams

Sometimes, I wonder
What is my dream?
What are dreams?

Are our dreams our ambitions?
Or are they our ultimate goal?

I don't know what my dream is
But then again,
How can I have a dream when I don't have a goal?

Or maybe my dream is to find a goal
Maybe my dream is to be somebody

I feel I've lost my identity while looking for dreams
And now I only have a lost wandering soul

Perhaps my dream is to find myself and become somebody
But how do you become somebody?

# Dreamworld

I'm all alone
Alone with my thoughts clouding my mind

My mind is full of things
Things that are dark and scary

But then my thoughts turn into a fantasy, a scenario
They make me believe I'm not alone

Everything seems so bright
And my mind is full of things again

But this time,
They are of love, happiness and joy

I feel I'm surrounded by people
I finally feel like dreams can come true

I live in a dreamworld and I'm happy
Because finally I'm somebody.

# A Wandering Soul

When I close my eyes, I feel like anything is possible
Like a wandering soul that can go anywhere

I can do anything I want
I can be anyone I want
I can be a character from a movie

I can be the actor, the director, the screenwriter and the producer
All at the same time
And I can create my own story
I can live the life anyone would desire

A life full of success and love.

# Success

Winter,
The month of cold and snow
Yet, the sky is blue

People are out on the streets
Taking in the freshness of the day
The birds are singing happily in the sun

I open my eyes and take in the beauty of nature
It seems like there is light everywhere
Even in the dark

This reality doesn't seem so harsh
The world seems peaceful
And success is within my hands.

# Shifts

Like the wind, life can shift into a million directions
One moment you are happy, seeking affections
And before you get immersed into a blissful life
You get seduced by the afterlife

The road to success seems endless
And I feel everything is senseless
My feet start to hurt
I am stuck in a silent desert

The world feels empty and I'm thirsty
I only see tall sandy dunes, the wind gets mighty
A bedouin stops me, telling me to follow him,
To see life again, to stop being so grim

Nothing to lose, I walk for hours again
But I feel nothing will be gained
But then I see it, an oasis, a fantasyland
A world where sadness is banned.

# Fantasyland

It's a warm summer day
Everyone is at the beach
Embracing the warmth of the sand,
the sound of the waves and the twinkling sun

Suddenly, a cold breeze runs through my skin
Unwillingly, my mind drifts to a cold fantasyland
Awed by the beauty of the snow,
I bravely take a step towards the white valley

I pass by penguins and polar bears
They wave, asking me to join them to sing jingle bells
The ambience is jolly, I feel merry and festive.
And I start dancing to the song of nature

Suddenly, the soft, cold breeze turns into a mighty wind
It overtakes the gentle sound of the trees
Feeling distressed and cold,
I try to find shelter within the endless white moonlit valley

Running through sharp icy shrubs,
I look for an exit
My skin feels cold, I wish I was at home
In my bed, snuggling in with my warm blankets

Lost in my thoughts,
The scenery of heavy snow changes
I find a cave hidden within the icy landscape
Relieved, I run inside and relax

I can't stop envisioning my soft and warm blankets at home.
Fantasy worlds may seem beautiful,
but there is nothing better than home.
With that thought, I wait for the storm to end

The land of soft snowflakes is disturbed by an intense snowstorm
The gentle sound of the breeze
turned into a heavy metal band's wild sound,
and I feel like screaming alongside them.

Afraid of the storm, I close my eyes,
I try to remember the sandy beach
the warmth of the turquoise waves of the sea
And the feeling of the warm sun rays on my skin

After what feels like centuries,
The concert of the snowstorm comes to an end
My skin feels warmer,
and I can hear the beautiful music of the waves

Slowly, I open my eyes
the sea is right in front of me
Feeling perplexed, I look around
All I can see is the vast sandy beach

I realise everything was just an illusion,
a fantasy created by a cold breeze on a summer day.
It seems like the wind, dreams and life are born.
Then, they grow, evolve, and create, until they come to an end.

# Reality

My eyes are finally open
The dream is over

My fantasy world is gone
One moment I was a successful, strong woman
And now I feel pathetic

My room is a mess
I feel cheated by life
And I feel useless

I was trying to be somebody
Somebody worthy
And I became the best version of myself

But I became someone that doesn't exist in reality
On the outside I looked fabulous and happy
But on the inside I was miserable and lonely

Still, for the first time I feel content
I finally feel alive
Because now I see the truth.

# Trying

People think reality is harsh
But now I realise, so are dreams

Thinking, contemplating, dreaming, wishing
We work so hard for an uncertain possibility

Sometimes it makes me think

Why are we trying?
Is it worth it?
Is there something better for us out there?
Is there something better than reality?

Maybe if I keep trying, I'll find a better reality.

# No Exit

I'm tired
I'm tired of trying to find the right path

I thought life would turn for the better if I started living in reality
But I'm so tired of people and society

And anyway, what is society?

I don't even want to bother with this anymore
I don't want to deal with anyone
I want to escape this constant trying to live

But I can't find an exit
I'm stuck until I can find my reality.

# A New Door

They say reality is boring
It is mundane and harsh

They say routine is lethal
It enslaves them to a never-ending cycle

People seek a high adrenaline lifestyle
They desire adventures

But isn't adventure part of reality?
Isn't routine part of life?

Getting lost in a fantasy land
Seeking for an exit

All these are part of life
They are a part of reality

You just need to create your reality
To find a new door to another reality

The secret is to remain yourself
To merge your new self with your old persona.

# **Running**

It's a sunny day
People are out on the streets
Birds are singing a spring song
Kids are anticipating the long-awaited summer holidays

Seeking for some peace and quiet
I'm off to the nearest park
I need to get away from my often-suffocating tiny room

I find a clearing amongst tall oaks and wild flowers
Squirrels are playing hide and seek
Seagulls are waiting for their next prey
Passers-by are lost in their little fantasy

Observing this tiny corner of the world
I get immersed into a dream world
I put on my favourite song
And close my eyes to get away from reality

I get lost in other lands
In a faraway kingdom
A world with no borders

A life with no worries

Immersed in a fantasy land again
I hear someone say,
"We gotta get away from here"
I open my eyes and I feel like running

So, I run
I run away
I run from my fantasy land
To get lost in a new reality.

# Lost

While trying to find myself
I lost my old self
With no identity
I felt useless

I messed up my life
I became a shell of a being
I felt like a robot

I was happy when other people were happy
I was sad when other people were sad
I couldn't show my real emotions
My only goal was to please others

While I was lost in an abyss
I became someone else
And that someone else stole my life

Now I feel like I can't restore what I lost
I'm trying to pick up the pieces of what was left of my fake persona

I'm fighting to get back my life
To live again

But my loved ones do not know me
They do not know my true self

And so, I feel broken again.

# A Broken Shell

Walking down to the beach
The street is filled with happy faces
On the corner of my eyes, I can see the glittery, shining golden sand

I can hear the sound of the waves breaking on the rocks
I feel a warm breeze brushing my hair
I feel the serenity of nature

The moment I arrive at the seducing beach, I take my shoes off
I feel a strong presence overtaking my body
I feel welcomed and loved

Suddenly, I hear loud voices
Looking around, I see a couple fighting
I feel discouraged

My moment of bliss breaks
I try to avoid their squabbling
I walk away and follow the scent of the sea

I find the perfect spot to enjoy the full view of the sand
merging with the sea
Like a kid, I play with the glittery sand
I try to find pretty rocks and shells

And then I see it
A broken shell
No, a beautiful fragment of a shell

Because I know no matter how broken people are
they can still overcome their difficulties,
they can get mended, live and love again.

# Selfish

Here I am,
Living the life, I always wanted
I feel strong and powerful
But life is still unfair and complicated
And I feel guilty
People around me seem miserable
No matter how hard I try to enjoy the beauty of the world
I keep seeing sadness
I don't know how to feel about the world anymore
I feel like a victim
I want to help
But instead of trying to resolve the world's problems
I just keep going and moving ahead
You may call me selfish
But I simply choose to be happy.

# How to Love

A small town, a tiny country
A loving family, a happy young girl
The reality was a dreamworld
And then reality tore the happiness apart

Living alone, brought sorrow, resentment and hate

Still on the road to discovery,
I learned that love doesn't die
I learned to appreciate my family and friends
I learned to cherish my memories, good and bad

Yet, I still struggle to love myself.

# Somebody to Love

Love, such a small word
But with so many hidden emotions inside

You are either born with love
Or you learn how to love

Tirelessly looking for your 'Once upon a time'
You often get in a story with no happy ending

Crying for love, smiling for love
Screaming loudly for love, speaking softly for love

You just want someone to love
Someone to give you a 'They lived happily ever after'.

# Perfect Match

Desiring the perfect partner
Someone to share your life with

A kind-hearted partner
A humble and kind person

Someone who gives love, safety and guidance
And someone who doesn't see only positiveness

The world is not always kind

I need someone who is strong,
Someone, who can stand up against the world with me
Someone, who is kind and helps those in need

And someone who knows how to keep smiling during tough times
Someone, who knows how to hold their dignity
Someone, who knows how to move on when needed.

# Find Somebody

A rare gemstone
A golden throne
A mysterious knight
Fighting in the night

A sweet girl
An eccentric earl
Elegant gown of silk
Bitter tea with milk

A bright smile
Off to a hopeless exile
Looking for somebody
Becoming somebody's

Falling in love
Choosing to love
Looking for a blessing
Getting a curse.

# Dinner

There is an empty bottle of wine
The Carbonaro's scent still lingers in the air
The kitchen is begging for attention

A couple is smiling, laughing
The quirky music of an out-of-tune piano fills the room
The promises for a better future go unsaid

The party goes on
They are only just getting by
But life is good.

# Abyss

There was a young man
He was standing on the edge
Feeling hopeless
Demons in his head were screaming profanities
They were teasing him, laughing at him
He feels like there is a hole in his soul
He's begging to piece him back together

His patience is waning
He feels angry
His rage is overtaking him
He steps away from the edge
He falls into an abyss
An abyss full of arms reaching out to him
They are dragging him away

He keeps falling
Until he hits rock bottom
He is crying
He wishes someone could hear him
But I am already tired

Tired of the rage, tired of the anger
I just want peace.

# A Simple Human

I don't want to feel like this
But I'm just a simple human
I can't control my feelings

I gave my all to another person
I shared my feelings, my story, my trust
And now, I feel disappointed and betrayed

Right now, I just want to disappear
I don't want to be here
I want to hide in a cave, get swept by a storm, get engulfed by the sea

I want to get lost in an icy landscape
Feel the cold breaking my body and mind
I don't want to feel anything anymore.

# Choosing to Love

You held my heart in your hands
Like it was just an old toy

Sitting in the deep dark
I waited for you to remember, I am just a human

But you threw me away like I was nothing
Feeling betrayed the earth cried for days

Howling wolves surrounded me in the dark
The earth started shaking like a leaf

Dense thunderstorm clouds covered the sky
But lightning kept showing me the way to love

You can't choose whom to fall in love with
But you can choose to love yourself.

# A Cloud

Everyone loves sunshine, clear skies and fresh air
But sometimes, I feel like I just need a cloud to give me rain to bloom

There was a time I was miserable
I was lost and alone
I made a lot of mistakes
My whole life was full of grey clouds and thunderstorms

I didn't ask for help
I thought I could find my way through the clouds by myself

Everyone kept trying to give me rainbows
But I insisted on holding on my cloud

It took me a long time but rain helped me to bloom
Pretty flowers started sprouting around me
And serenity surrounded me

A path of daisies, lilies and peonies appeared before me
I didn't know where it would lead me
But I just hoped I'll finally arrive at the place I belong.

# Keep Living

The wind is blowing
The trees are dancing calmly to the soothing beat of a waltz
And I'm lost

I'm lost within fluffy clouds
I'm lost within tall trees
I'm lost within deep valleys

But I'm finally moving again
I'm flying away to other lands
And with the rainbow as my compass
I give a chance to myself.

# Egocentric

The sun is out, and so am I
With my best smile on, I walk confidently
I dance to my favourite's song rhythm
And I feel beautiful

People are staring
People are smiling at my silly moves
Others feel threatened by my happiness
And I don't care

Then he walks up to me
He smiles, he says hello
He says he loves that, "I'm in my own world"
I say thank you and continue living in my own world.

# Eccentric

New life, new look, new self
I feel different,
Like an actor impersonating a new character

The script seems interesting
But I want it to be eccentric
Not just another boring story

I want to be the rainbow on a rainy day
I want to be the only light in a dark night
I want to be a yellow daisy in a field of white daisies

I want to be the colourful person amongst millions of grey people.

# **Greediness**

Once you find your true self, you can't go back
But humans are greedy

Although you still wish you can be different
Sometimes you want to be like the rest

You want to blend in the crowd
You want your colourful persona to look like any others

To create a soothing harmony
To become one clan, one family, one story.

# Waves

With the waves, I want to be swept away,
but instead, I feel enslaved by the sand
I miss floating in the water,
I miss flying away with the wind

My roots are getting stronger,
but no matter how tall I get, I can't fly
I became trapped in a life I was meant to have
But never wanted
I stay because it is easy, it is cosy, it is familiar

But I miss floating in the water,
I miss flying away with the wind.

# Trapped

Tall skyscrapers reach the blue sky
Proud and imposing
People are taking over the streets
Hurried and expressionless
Buses carry millions of tourists
They are excited and full of wonder
Tamed waters proudly embrace the city
Calmly and peacefully
Fast and large waggons lure me beneath the earth
To Tartarus
To get silky tunics and fancy wine
I feel important and independent
But then I end up at an ordinary pub
It's cosy and welcoming
I end up watching various people of different coloured shirts
running and chasing
People are enjoying the show
But then I wonder
For whom are they so excited about?
Who are they really watching?
I feel the people staring
I think they are mocking me

I feel like a prey
I wonder, why am I here?
I laugh it off and continue observing, waiting
I feel life running at a fast pace
But I can feel the city's immortality
It won't wait for me to decide or understand
It is a dream city for many
But once here, you get enslaved by the city's brightness
And sometimes life takes you away
To escape this fate, I go back at the wagon beneath the earth
I search for the next destination
Hoping for freedom and serenity.

# Nostalgia

The rain falls softly
Feeling bold
I walk on a dimmed road
My shadow follows me quietly

The glinting lights hide my tears
Music is ringing in my ears
"I'm going home, to the place I belong"
But everything feels wrong

Gentle pitter-patter follows me
From solitude I flee
Seeking a new home
I can't wait to roam

Nostalgia breaks my heart
Nostalgia soothes my heart
Another home, another love
Another place, another time

Walking in the shimmering moonlight
My smile is bright

My tears fade away
And I'm on my way.

# The Light

The light will guide you to the end of the tunnel
The light will bring you a joyful and pure life
But life is much more complicated

Sometimes, we arrive at the end of the tunnel,
And we are not satisfied

The question is,
Should we move forward,
or go back and start again?

I can't find a correct answer

Mistakes are part of life
The only thing I can do is move in the best way I know
After all, trying is what matters

Even if others keep telling me of my mistakes or wrong choices
I won't falter

I'll do what is best for me
I am not going to lose my dreams and hope
I will keep going towards the light and beyond.

# Another Chance

I messed up again
Everything was going well, even perfect
But nothing ever stays perfect
My shyness and insecurity held me back
And I messed up my second chance

I don't feel discouraged
I can still move on
I still feel strong and confident
Because my life is now in my hands
And I can still continue my journey

I just feel sorry for messing up
I feel sorry that I still need time
Time to figure out how to be me, which path I should follow
and where I belong
I just hope one day I will find the answers I need.

# The Brightest Star

I won't apologise
I don't care if they stop and stare

I want a good life
I want to feel again
I want to know I lived with no regrets

Wherever I go,
I'll live in my way
I'll follow my dreams

And if I'm surrounded by darkness
I'll look for the brightest star.

# Darkness

I keep following the brightest star
But sometimes
Darkness takes over the streets

People walk in a fast pace
Their eyes seem avoidant
Still, they keep walking at a steady pace

And just like that, we move on
We get taken by darkness
We pass through life
And sometimes we forget how to live.

# Pretending

I can't pretend anymore
I'm tired
I feel lonely
I hate myself

I always motivate myself by saying,
"It's okay, everything will be fine in the end",
But I can't pretend anymore
And I don't know what I should do

I am much better now
The person I became is the best version I could be
Yet, there is still a hole in my heart

Perhaps it's because I feel guilty
I feel guilty for lying and pretending to be okay
Maybe I should just enjoy the ride
And perhaps somehow everything will be alright.

# Be Yourself

I always felt like the odd person
The weird one who doesn't fit in the world

I've always been a curious person
I wanted to know everything
So, I sought after the truth of the universe

I distanced myself from the world
And kept looking for answers

In the end, I felt isolated and didn't get any correct answers

The only one I found is
Be You
Be yourself and live as yourself
And the right people will come to you.

# **Different**

Sometimes I wish I wasn't so different
One moment I'm confident and powerful
I'm surrounded by love and I am fulfilled

And then the next,
I see everyone leaving me behind

I told them to wait for me, to be patient
But instead, they moved on

I don't blame them for it
But I wish they could wait
I wish they could wait until I feel comfortable and ready.

# Reflection

Drifting into a restless sleep
Counting rocky mountain sheep
Running through golden fields
Reaching unsolved mindfields

In the artificial lake
My reflection seems like a mistake
Everything feels like a lie
Please hear my cry

Mountains stand tall, imposing
Surrounded by hatred and loathing
All the deception is exposed
A cacophony is composed

My reflection shifts into a mirage
Giving me an abstract message
Find a magical mirror
End your trial and error.

# The Biggest Mistake

The biggest mistake is giving up

I gave up on myself
I gave up on the world
I gave up on life

I thought I was not good enough
But now I know better
I'm good enough

Even if I'm slow
I will get to the end of my path
I'll achieve my dreams

No matter what others say
I will not stay silent anymore
I will not try to be something I am not
I will not pretend to be someone else
I will embrace my oddities and rule the world.

# A Quiet Volcano

You think I don't know how you see me?

Some people call it outdated,
others say that just how the mind works
But I call it wrong

You look at me as if I'm an object that already belongs to you
You talk to me as if I'm your inferior and I need to learn from you

I told you many times to look at me straight in the eyes
I told you to talk to me as your equal
You always laugh and said I'm too sensitive

At the end I exploded like a quiet volcano
I snapped and screamed and cried
And you said I was mad

The next day you stopped looking at me
You behaved as if I didn't exist

I don't care that you are out of my life,
But I care that you didn't change
That you still behave the same way

Some people say your behaviour is outdated,
Others simply say that's how the mind works
But I call it wrong.

# An Independent Volcano

I don't care that you are out of my life
The world doesn't go around you

And guess what
I won't stop going around the world because of you

I'll stop thinking of your unacceptable behaviour and I'll keep living
It's time for me to live for myself and not others

But I've been thinking

If I don't care about you
And clearly you don't care about me
Why is it such a big deal to you if I'm different?

I live my life and I'm happy
I speak my truth
And I don't hide myself anymore
Because now, I know that
there is nothing wrong with my personality or self-identity

Instead of trying to get my attention with your attitude
Try to do the same thing as me
Follow my footsteps
And try to self-discover yourself.

# Disappointment

I worked so hard to find my truth
I searched and struggled and cried
And I'm finally happy with my inner and outer self

But now I see the pettiness of people
I see how they don't care about an individual's truth

They seem acceptant
But then they step on your truth as if it's just an old doormat

They step on you to open a new door
A supposedly better door

But they are only looking for answers
Because you are not who they thought you are anymore

Now I just feel disappointed
And I regret sharing my truth.

# A volcano

Sometimes, I feel like an active volcano
I want to explode,
I want to cover everything with lava,
And spread ashes all over the streets

I want to be gloomy and spooky

And sometimes I want to be an inactive volcano
I want to know that I have the power to spread fear
But to also make life around me bloom,
To make people feel safe and happy

I want to be bright and cheerful.

# **Ironic**

So many expectations

People always saw me as someone who can do anything
But I am just an ordinary human being
There are things I can't possibly do
I am not a superhuman
Yet people still expected me to do the impossible

Now, I know I should only follow my intuition
I should follow my own expectations
I should create my own path
But now, people tell me it is impossible to do that
Ironic, right?

# Slow

They say I'm slow
I'm in my late 20s and I still feel like a child
Everyone around me is growing, developing, transforming
And I'm just a child

I'm my mother's daughter
I'm my father's pride
I'm the universe's child

I may be slow
But I walk at a steady pace.

# The Universe

It is Monday afternoon
People are on the streets
Walking, running, biking, enjoying the rare warm day

The sun rays pierce the clouds
The sky is a canvas with beautiful blues shades
The sea is wild and the tide high

I sit alone gazing at the sea
People pass by me, some look at me curiously,
some greet me, some smile at me

I am my self's only company
But the sea's presence is loud
I feel surrounded by the universe.

# Hope

The sound of the sea always gives me strength

The feel of a million tiny rocks and crystals on my skin
Keep me connected to the earth
It helps me ground myself
It helps me stay aware of reality

Seeing the deep blue of the sea intertwined with the light blue of the sky,
gives me hope,
It helps me get lost in the dreamworld
It helps me visualise my dreams.

# **Midnight**

It's past midnight
People pass by me laughing, chatting
Living in a superficial happiness

I walk alone with my shadow following me
Telling me to be careful of lingering shadows

It's easy to get absorbed by darkness
It's easy to get distracted by noise

The night is tempting me
It wants me to go back
To old and undesired habits and feelings

I need to be stronger
I need to find my light
I need the sun.

# Sun

The sun is always watching over us

When we feel cold and hopeless,
the sun is there
waiting and asking us to leave behind the past

The sun is strong and mighty
It can burn everything within a short distance

Yet, when it's cold outside,
the bright sun makes us feel warm, happy and blissful

The glorious sun is everything we hope for.

# Glory

Intoxicated I sing, I dance
Closing my eyes, I feel the rhythm

All my senses are heightened
I can hear the war cry ringing in my ears

I'm surrounded by madness,
I feel besieged

My mind is blinded by bright lights
My body is craving for a touch

The sun is gone
The moon, my only guidance

I seek for glory
But I only got pathetic worshippers

I feel rage
I feel sad.

# Apology

I'm sorry for what I become

I lost my soul
In a world that burns

I was looking for forgiveness
But only found disappointed eyes

I desired glory
But only found greedy eyes

I was seeking for undying love
But only found possessiveness

I was waiting for the day the heavens' gate would open
I was waiting for the day the ocean would split into two
I was waiting for the divine to descend on earth

But the world only kept burning
And I kept apologising .

# Emotions

Everyone desires the burning feeling of excitement
The warm temperature of the sun
The passion of a fire

But I feel an overwhelm of emotions
They keep dragging me into the deep waters of the ocean

People say these emotions are weak
But the same people are fearful of water

With large waves, an ocean can take the anger and the rage away

Water can take you away to different lands and worlds
Water can teach you resilience and hope
Water can give you life
Water can save you.

# A Cold Night

At home, I feel warm and cosy
But today, I feel suffocated
I feel like I'm going out of oxygen

I decide to go out for a stroll in the city
It's a cold night
but the city is lively

I get immersed by the sounds of the people
I can hear chatter, laughing,
glasses clinking, songs mingling together
a dog barking, a woman yelling

And before I know it, I am at the coast again
I can hear the waves going wild,
It seems as if they are laughing in an evil manner
Mocking the people, provoking them to go for a swim

Still, I continue to walk on the waves' beat
It's a windy winter night
But I feel content and warm by being surrounded by water
I feel like I'm finally home.

# Keep Moving

This is not the end
I made many mistakes
But now I can stand again
I can face the world again
I'm not going to lose again

I was in an abyss
But I got out
And I won't let anything stop me now

Anywhere my heart desires
Whenever my mind decides
I'll keep moving
I'll keep being myself
I'll keep writing and speaking my truth.

# Utopia

The world has called my name
I have nothing to fear now

I feel nothing and everything
Is this what it feels like to dream again?

I feel like I lost all my senses
I feel my body, my mind, my soul moving

They are moving towards a better ending
They are moving towards utopia

I keep moving, walking towards the light
Searching for my euphoria.

# The Queen

Dreams may only be a fantasy
but everyone desires to live in a dreamworld.

Every morning, everyone waits for the night to come
Everyone waits for the time they can just dream

Every night, the stars bring shining light to the world.
And the longing for a dreamworld ends

The bright stars fill the dark void with hope.
People joyfully dance, sing, fall in love

The night is glowing with vibrant colours
And the people wish upon a star for a happy ending

But I am just a dim star,
My light is dull, my presence forgotten

The seven heavens despise my existence
The seven oceans complain for my incompetence

Insecurity overwhelms me
My dreamworld of brightness is crumbling

Unwanted, unloved, my days are empty
Dangerously, the void is dragging me away

The night has come again, I feel like crying
But then the sun appears before me

"Child, don't cry, you may shine dimly now"
"But you are not just a star, one day you'll grow to be the moon"

"One day not only will you bring hope to the people"
"You'll bring happiness, love and life"

Encouraged, my faded light flickers in the sky
Until the heavens, the oceans and the people see me

Today, I shine more brightly than anyone in the night
The universe is covered with my dazzling light

My dreamworld is not a fantasy anymore
It is my reality

Because I am the moon
The Queen of the sky.